Wild Geese

Wild Geese

THEODORE H. BANKS, JR.

NEW HAVEN · YALE UNIVERSITY PRESS
LONDON · HUMPHREY MILFORD · OXFORD UNIVERSITY PRESS
MDCCCCXXI

ACKNOWLEDGMENTS.

GRATEFUL acknowledgments are made to *Everybody's Magazine* for permission to reprint poems included in this volume.

TO MY MOTHER.

Thine is the beauty of the summer stars
  Gathered within a fern-fringed pool,
When not a ripple mars
  Its surface cool.

Thou art as fragrant as the peach-tree's bloom,
Bending beneath so rich a store
That there is hardly room
  For one bud more.

Thy grace is as the grace of ripening wheat
That to the wind's soft wooing yields,
Sending the shadows fleet
  Across the fields.

The glint of sunny waters is thy smile.
Thy laughter brings as dear delight
As birds' clear singing while
  The dawn grows bright.

Thou couldst not but be fair, for thy pure soul
Transfigures thee with an excess
Of light, an aureole
  Of holiness.

Yet thou art not a pale and pensive saint
Dreaming thy cloistered life away,
Despising the restraint
  Of this dull clay.

Nay, rather dost thou glory in thy flesh,
Wearing it proudly as a queen,
For 'tis a garment fresh
   And bright and clean.

Nor dost thou like a bee suck only sweet,
Or dwell in selfishness apart,
Not knowing weary feet
   Or aching heart.

Thou seekest sorrow with grave, tender eyes
And gentle touch that soothes and heals.
All human miseries
   Thy spirit feels.

As radiant as a star, yet not remote,
Clothed with its splendor, not its snow,
When it gleams keen-rayed, afloat
   In the sunset glow,

Thou hast no setting; for when thou dost pass
Beyond our mortal vision, dead,
Thou wilt make bright the grass
   Where angels tread.

CONTENTS.

PART I. LYRICS.

Wild Geese	13
The Return	14
The Tokens	15
The Awakening	16
The Mogi Road	17
"As I Sat Dreaming"	18
Prayer	19
November	20
"A Sea-Change"	21
Tempest	22

PART II. SONNETS.

In Memoriam. W. H. Branham:	
I.	25
II.	25
III.	26
IV.	26
To Buckner Pearson Sholl	27
Beyond	28
The Heritage	29
Victory	30
Autumn	31
To Death:	
I.	32
II.	32
III.	33

PART III. THE VIGIL   37

PART IV. THE FOUR WINDS.

Summer	47
Autumn	48
Winter	50
Spring	52

PART V. THE ALTAR CANDLE   56

PART I.
LYRICS.

WILD GEESE.

Wild geese are flying, crying, flying,
   Sweeping over rice fields, swift across the sun,
Black against the west where the day is dying,
Winging to the northward till the day is done.

Wild geese are calling, falling, calling,
Swirling down clamorous among the tasselled reeds,
Settling in the rushes where the yellow river's crawling,
Sinking into silence as the night succeeds.

Wild geese are springing, winging, springing,
Rising from the rushes, for the dawn is nigh,
Flying to the northward their wild cry ringing,
Mounting like a matin-song beneath the flushing sky.

THE RETURN.

WHEN I return, let us be very still;
    One searching, passionate, soul-sufficing glance,
And a deep silence. Mirth would become us ill,
Because of the unnumbered graves of France,
Where love lies buried on each trampled hill.

THE TOKENS.

I KNOW by these that she cannot have died:
　　The woodland quiet, the sparkle of the sea,
The flutter of leaves, the flooding of the tide,
Earth's lure and loveliness and mystery;
For all these things she loved, and these abide.

Nor is her spirit, clad in gentleness,
　　Courage and courtliness and ancient grace,
Less than the beauty of the stars, or less
Than fading light that touched her tender face,
The twilight calm, or the low wind's caress.

The dark pine woods, secluded and secure
Against the world, the majesty that moved
On the tempestuous ocean, and the pure,
Pale light of dawning: all these that she loved
Were transient, earthly things; and these endure.

THE AWAKENING.

When I shall wake from life, and in surprise
    Behold the brilliance of more spacious skies
Whose splendor is yet terrible and strange,
Then will you come with welcome in your eyes.

Then will you fold me close in tender arms,
And with your cherishing touch that heals and charms
Lull me as in the golden days of earth,
Shield me from fear of unknown, heavenly harms.

Then will the music of your speaking fill
The solitude to comfort me, and thrill
My soul with sense of old companionship,
Waking loved echoes that have long been still.

Then will your yearning bosom bend to mine,
Your heart beat to my heart, your clear eyes shine
With light will make the heaven seem friendly earth,
The loving light that once made earth divine.

Then will your soul, dauntless and undismayed,
Lead me among the wonders, wide displayed,
Till paradise will seem almost as sweet
As that wild, woodland path where once we strayed.

THE MOGI ROAD.

A GLOW of lanterns on the tall bamboo,
   Slender, tapering, smooth and green,
The branches like a feathery screen
Against uncertain stars that glimmer through;

The fields seen dimly in the lantern glow;
And through the darkness redolent
Low, haunting flute notes that lament
The love and the romance of long ago.

"AS I SAT DREAMING."

As I sat dreaming in my room
   The shadows gathered and the gloom;
There was no sound except the rain
That tapped against the window-pane,
Like to a phantom lonely there
In rising wind and darkening air.
I did not heed the night, nor hear
The tapping of those hands of fear;
My spirit walked in splendor, far
Beyond the bound of sun or star,
Treading where every poet trod
Since the first song rose up to God;
Saw for a golden moment's space
Eternal beauty's matchless face;
Heard for an instant, clear and strong,
The marvel of immortal song.
And so I did not know the rain
Was beating on the window-pane.

PRAYER.

Richly the tapers glimmer, and their gold
   Floods all the chapel: sculptured altar screen,
The high, oak pews with carven ornament,
The deep-resounding organ, in whose pipes
Glitter a thousand candles, and the altar,
Pure and unveinèd marble. There the blaze
Is brightest, and the golden crucifix
Burns like a flame; and there you stand, white-robed,
While at your feet the choir chants, silver-tongued,
And the great organ throbs in ecstasy.
And when the last amen has died away
Among the shadows of the vaulted roof,
Humbly you kneel and offer up your prayer.

But I in silence walk beneath the stars.

NOVEMBER.

THE long, bare beach and the ebbing tide,
　　The creeping fog on the face of the sea;
And all my dreams that the world denied
Rising to mock my misery.

The water winding across the sand,
The low waves lapping upon the shore;
And fires that have left but a blackened brand,
And hopes that my heart shall hold no more.

The dull clouds driving across the sky,
Heavy with threat of the hissing rain;
And the lilt of laughter, long gone by,
Of lips that shall never smile again.

The sea wind sweeping, wet and cold,
A flurry of sea birds fleeting past;
And desire for the day that pain is old
And rest is come at last.

"A SEA-CHANGE."

The snow falls silently, and brings
New loveliness to common things,
And gives to every ugly place
Still forms of beauty and of grace,
Making the busy, bustling street
A solitude where phantoms meet
And dimly pass on muffled feet.

And could I to like beauty turn
The passions that within us burn,
The grief, the weariness, the strife,
The tumult of our daily life,
Then in a hushed world you would see
How strangely altered we should be,
How clothed in lasting mystery.

TEMPEST.

Savage the sea leaped high; on the rocks plunged ponderous breakers,
Hoary with streaking of spray; and the surges with foam swift flying
Moaned by the bases of sheer cliffs, smitten and shaken with tumult,
Furious sprang at the land, and rebounded in wildest confusion
Twisted and tossed in their clutches the sinuous ribbons of sea-weed
Torn from the still, dark bed of the sea by the might of the tempest.
There in the deeps and the hollows of white crests curling and combing
Darted on flickering pinions a petrel, intrepidly flying.
Hurled from the heart of the east, huge thunder-clouds swept o'er the ocean,
Trailing their fringes of rain with its low hiss lost in the clamor.
Loud was the voice of the wind; and the sunlight in fugitive flashes
Glorious shot through the clouds with their clefts and their terrible caverns,
Gleamed for a time and was gone, as the clouds came sullen together.
Trees in the stream-filled gorges dividing precipitous headlands
Bent with their boughs that were wrenched by the wind as it swooped through the valleys,
Bent to the banks of the brooks as they rushed in their mad haste seaward.
Full in the sting of the rain and the fury of wind I was standing;
There by the ruinous waste of the ocean I stood in amazement,
Wondered and worshipped in sight of the grandeur of God the All-mighty.

PART II.
SONNETS.

IN MEMORIAM.
WILLIAM H. BRANHAM,
MASTER AT ST. PAUL'S SCHOOL.

I.

I could not write to you when you were dying,
Even to cheer you, of the trivial things
That summer to an idle schoolboy brings;
I could not speak so when I knew you lying
Within death's shadow, bravely death defying;
Nor had I skill to touch more solemn strings.
So was I speechless with the grief that wrings
A spirit impotent, the end descrying.
Boyish I wrote at last, impulsively,
And spoke my sorrow from a loaded heart,
Hoping to lighten you of some small part
Of the dark burden of your misery.
And then you tore my very soul apart
For you, the dying, wrote to comfort me.

II.

I could not speak then for I had no skill,
Nor knew the courageous spirit I had lost;
Now I guess darkly what the struggle cost,
When with your splendid strength and dauntless will
You met death face to face and fought until
The body broke. So in autumnal frost
I have seen oaks, their naked branches tossed
Against the heavens on a windy hill.
I cannot think the everlasting rest
And quiet of heaven is a just reward
For your keen spirit tempered like a sword;
Still would you seek to win a distant goal,
Still journey onward in a noble quest.
Strife is the guerdon for so strong a soul.

III.
Often the iron of the winding stair
Clattered, as hastily with lusty shout
I mounted to your door, and paused without,
Till to your welcoming cry I entered there,
To ask for comfort in a schoolboy care,
To seek solution of a weighty doubt,
Or joyously to say the buds were out
And spring was coming with the quickened air.
Youth pays no heed to death, nor understands
That the day's happiness will ever change,
Or love and friendship fail; and I, a boy,
Held those dear moments in unfeeling hands,
Scattered and squandered them in thoughtless joy.
How precious are they now, how sad, how strange.

IV.
Your room was a sure refuge where I fled
To lose my grief in the unfailing cheer
Your kindness gave to me, past speaking dear;
For there I talked as friend to friend, instead
Of boy to man; or when the day was dead
In quiet contentment watched the stars appear,
You in your armchair, reading from Lanier,
Blue clouds of eddying smoke above your head.
I never thought those days would vanish soon,
Those joyous days of friendship, and of life
Wherein the past and future had no part.
Now after many years, a certain tune
Of your belovèd Spain cuts like a knife,
And fragrance of tobacco twists my heart.

TO BUCKNER PEARSON SHOLL.

UPRIGHT he stands and clean and straight and strong,
   Like a high springing tree, hill crowning, where
Only the sunlight and the clear, cool air
Surround him ever. Far above the throng,
Among the gathered glories that belong
To the wide heaven, splendid he towers there;
And in his face his soul is featured fair,
The soul of Galahad who did no wrong.
Through the far fields of France he went his way,
Dwelling with ghastliness and girt with death,
Silent and steady-eyed; and homeward brought
Cleanness of heart like dawn of summer day,
Freshness of spirit like the north wind's breath,
And beauty like a sword blade finely wrought.

BEYOND.

IMMEASURABLY below, the planets swing,
And all the spirits sit without a sound;
The peace of countless ages wraps them round;
The old stars fade, and others blazing bring
Tidings of new worlds of God's fashioning.
So bide they in tranquillity profound,
Deep in the heart of heaven without a bound,
Distant beyond the mind's imagining.
Yet not so distant that there cannot come,
Faint for a moment like a pulse of air,
Troubling the quietude eternal, some
Old, half-forgotten human grief or joy:
A young girl smiling as she combed her hair;
Or a child weeping by a broken toy.

THE HERITAGE.

Ye who have looked at death with laughing glance,
　　Dreamed and beheld your dreams resplendent rise,
And known transforming love that never dies,
Have wrought what will endure beyond mischance
With lives where death was but a circumstance;
For where each of the splendid fallen lies
Honor and hope and fearlessness arise
Like a rich incense from the fields of France.
For me a nobler earth, a vaster heaven
Ye fashioned with the glory of your days,
And gave immortal men and deeds to sing;
Save that I cannot give as ye have given,
And idle seems the shaping of sweet lays,
And making rhymes a poor and futile thing.

VICTORY.

Not like the beast, O God, not like the beast!
Let me not fling away the conscience gleams
Lighting the dark, my spirit-stirring dreams
And star-fixed vision for a gross flesh-feast.
I stand at the flushed gateway of the east;
Round me the light of youth's fresh morning streams;
The richest gifts of life are mine, it seems,
And with the best I would not change for least.
Earth claims her sensuous due of life and death;
Yet, if I yield not wholly to her lure,
I at the last triumphant shall arise;
And though I vanish like a frosty breath,
I shall outstrip the sun, outsoar the skies,
And when the stars are dead I shall endure.

AUTUMN.

The oak that towers where the rock ridge ends
　In rich autumnal pomp of red and gold,
Single and stately like a king of old,
Before the first, keen wind of winter bends;
And its great, rugged arms upflinging sends
Showering the leaves in eddies manifold,
As one who struggles from a cloak's thick fold
And unencumbered with the foe contends.
So may my soul, fronting eternity,
Steadfast and silent, face to face with God,
There in its being's frigid autumn fling
Its clinging cerements to the stiffened sod;
Stand naked and unashamed, and like the tree
Be clothed with ampler foliage in the spring.

TO DEATH.

I.

O Death, whose dark wing overshadows all,
   Whose steady, passionless, inscrutable eyes
Look coldly down on life's divine surprise,
On the heaped riches of life's festival,
How mighty art thou! at whose whispered call
We leave our dearest treasures, and arise,
And journey forth to that far land which lies
Wrapped in the dark that overshadows all.
O Death, before whose feet all life is bowed
How weak and witless art thou! for we see
Behind the gloom of thy close-gathered shroud
The blazing brilliance of the life to be
That glows unquenchable, as from a cloud
The raying sun shines out triumphantly.

II.

I listened when men spoke of Death, and heard
Of his transcendent might and majesty,
His mercy and his magnanimity
To those in pain; of sluggish spirits stirred
To action by his peremptory word;
Of lasting glory none could give save he;
Of knighthood and enduring dignity
That but one royal touch of his conferred.
Yet when I saw Death sitting in *her* place,
A shrunken figure crouched beside the fire,
Unmoved by passion, cold to all desire,
Shrouding with sable hood his fleshless face,
I saw no state or splendor of a king
In that ungainly, sightless, shrivelled thing.

III.
Silent along a summer-shadowed road
I walked with Death at my right hand. I knew
That he could still the wind that wandered through
The quiet lanes, could stay the stream that flowed
Beneath the trees, could blast their mellowing load
That at his touch would shrivel as the dew
Melts in the light of morning, and I knew
He could revoke all things that life bestowed.
All this I knew, yet fearlessly I turned
And full in his unswerving pathway stood,
That even for a moment I might peer
Beneath the shrouding darkness of his hood;
And deep within his angry eyes there burned
A sullen shame and an undying fear.

PART III.
THE VIGIL.

set her by to watch, and set her by to weepe."
—Faerie Queene.

THE VIGIL.

Through the great window opening on the west
  Came the deep crimson of departing day,
Flushing the cold hands crossed upon his breast,
Where with closed eyes the Queen's young lover lay,
Flooding the chamber for its little stay
  With beauty fitter for a marriage bed,
  Quickening with warmth the cold cheeks, ashen gray,
  Staining the covering and the couch one red,
And making pale the tapers ranged about his head.

Beside him a black-mantled, silent nun
  Knelt motionless; a pulse of evening air
Fluttered the candles; slowly, one by one,
The shadows gathered and grew long, save where
The last light of the sun, surpassing fair,
  Touched his still figure and his face serene.
  Then through the silence that was sovereign there
  Sounded a hurrying of feet unseen,
An ever-growing murmur and a cry, "The Queen!"

Suddenly were the doors flung wide apart;
  A burst of tumult and they shut again.
There was the Queen alone; against her heart
As though against unutterable pain
Seeking to quiet its throbbing all in vain,
  Her hands were pressed. Right regal from her head
  To the last jewel of her jeweled train
  She stood, stone still, and gazed upon the bed;
Only her white lips, anguished, stiffly whispered, "dead."

In the broad shaft of slowly fading light,
  Amid the darkness and the gathering gloom
And the deep shade of close-enfolding night,
Creeping about her like a stealthy doom,
Flamelike she stood; and like the broadening bloom,
  The kindling dawn-flush of triumphant day
  Fired with her fervor the still, sombre room,
  Scattered the shadows that about her lay
With her resplendent beauty's overmastering sway.

Then to the kneeling nun, who in surprise
  Paused in the telling of her rosary
  And from the dead raised her untroubled eyes,
  The Queen spake as befitted royalty
  (Only her pale lips trembled), "Leave us. We
  Keep here to-night our vigil in your place."
  Whereat the other rose up wonderingly
  And making obeisance, left her; for a space
She moved not, while the light grew less upon her face.

And then the mighty Queen who moonlike shone
  In sovereign splendor great and glorified,
  Moving august, majestic and alone,
  Among the lesser stars half deified,
  Vanished and left a woman; all her pride,
  Disdain and dignity and scorn were swept
  Before the full flood of her passion's tide.
  There at her dead love's feet she fell, and crept
Against his breast, and clasped his hands, and sadly wept

Long hours she lay there till her tears were dry,
  Stroking his forehead, whispering his name,
  Sobbing her grief out; while the evening sky
  Faded to utter darkness and became
  Glorious with starlight, while the taper-flame
  Deepened and ripened into glowing gold,
  While from the dark, tree-shaded garden came
  The chirp of crickets, smell of the fresh mould,
And the full fragrance of the blossoms manifold.

At length she rose, and with white, trembling hands
  Stripped off the jewels of her rich attire,
  Heavy with princely spoil of ravaged lands:
  Diamonds that flamed with a great city's fire,
  Pearls shimmering with murdered men's desire,
  Rubies that glistened with an emperor's blood,
  The ancient treasure of a funeral pyre;
  Loosened the fastenings of her hair and stood
With tresses flowing free, the sign of maidenhood.

"So I have dóne with sovereignty," she said,
  "And with the royalty that came between
  My love and me; now that my love is dead
  I have enough of pride of place, I ween;
  The mighty magic of the name of 'Queen'
  Has lost the virtue that it had of late;
  Queenhood is hateful to me, for I have seen
  The bitterness of majesty and state,
And know how sad it is and lonely to be great.

"I am become a woman once again,
  A queen no longer, yet will never be
  Free from my bitter penitence and pain,
  Free from my torturing regret or free
  From my intolerable memory."
  Soft as the night wind her voice died away,
  And in the silence she gazed dreamily
  At the deep-shadowed garden as it lay
Before her in the young-lived loveliness of May.

Slowly she sank down and sat heedless there
  In the still, starry night that like a shroud
  Clung close about her; with her loosened hair
  Gleaming like some bright, sun-enkindled cloud,
  Her white hands listless, and her fair head bowed
  That bent not with the weight of destinies,
  And her pale face, imperious and proud,
  Saddened and softened by her mourning eyes
Haunted with shapes of dreams and ghosts of memories.

Visions of new-green meadow and clear sun
  And a young soul that looked with wakening eyes
  On the world's wonder, pure heart scarce begun
  To feel the fires of deepening passion rise
  Like springing sunbeams to the morning skies,
  Bright with the beauty of the day to be.
  Love filled her spirit with a dim surmise:
  The tempest's first light touch upon the tree,
The gathering wind on the ungovernable sea.

Then in her brooding, verdant summer brought
   The peaceful days that like deep waters flow
Silently by, and in her heart she thought,
   "Before the rose has faded I will show
Some little sign that he mayhap will know
   I love him." Smiling for pure joy she went
Along the vivid garden, stooping low
   To raise some stem with weight of blossoms bent
With gentle touch that gave new life and hue and scent.

And on a day all fresh from recent rain,
   Sweet with the smell of earth and leaves washed clean,
Sunlike she moved among the flowers again,
   Softly as southern wind she went between
Them thinking, "Here where the tall lilies lean
   Together I will yield me." Thither came
Her lover where she lingered half unseen,
   Upon his lips the longing of her name,
And in his questing eyes the light of leaping flame

(Eyes closed forever in the candle light,
   And lips once eloquent with passion, cold
As the white moon slow-rising through the night).
   Then mid the shadows of her memories old
Came flash of jewels and swift gleam of gold,
   And courtiers bowing ceremoniously,
Bringing her splendor, stateliness untold,
   Dominion mighty as the sweeping sea,
Sceptre and diadem of thronèd majesty.

Before her rose with royal circumstance
   Kingdoms and realms and ancient emperies
Golden with legend and with old romance,
   Magnificent with song of centuries,
Bastioned with dreams and walled with memories
   Of long-gone glory and of dead desire:
All-ruling Rome, Persian Persepolis,
   Babylon and Nineveh, far-sailing Tyre,
And long-beleaguered Ilium, red crowned with fire.

And the fair, fabled Queens, whose very names
   Make music, rose before her, shining clear
   Through the deep darkness of old time like flames:
   Helen of Troy, Iseult and Guinevere,
   And Cleopatra, marvelous with sheer
   And splendid beauty; and a glowing throng
   Thick as the shadows when the night is near,
   Great kings and lords and princes who belong
To immemorial story and to age-old song.

As thus she mused, the moon high risen shone
   Upon her like a benediction, where
   With heart full sorrowing she sat alone,
   And made a saintly silver round her hair;
   On her dark, downcast eyes and bosom bare
   Its tranquil, cold caressing softly fell,
   As she sat deeply dreaming, unaware,
   Still wrapped in brooding, folded in the spell
Of joy close treasured and old hope remembered well.

Once more the summer blossomed at her feet,
   While through her soul like a resistless tide
   Swept high ambition and desire most meet
   For a great queen; before her new-born pride
   Her love, young, timid, half-reluctant died
   Like a pale star before the rush of day.
   Then from the garden, flushed and eager-eyed,
   Vestured in beauty like the rich array
Of dawning sun, she moved majestic on her way.

And in the morningtide of her delight,
   Her virgin dignity and honors new,
   Her unaccustomed majesty and might
   Made fair her ways before her like the hue
   Of newly budded blossoms fresh with dew;
   For in her heart bloomed happiness full-blown,
   And like a flower, content within her grew,
   And round her like a halo joyance shone
As in her maiden state she moved apart, alone.

Yet as the freshness of the morning dies
   When the swift splendor of the dawn is spent,
   So died her perfect peace; for vague surmise,
   Disquietude and nameless discontent,
   Strange restlessness and longing eloquent
   Disturbed the deep of her tranquillity;
   As in a spot, secluded, redolent
   Of long, warm, golden noon sounds distantly
The sweep and surge and tumult of the troubled sea.

Then suddenly she learned that he had died
   And her dim love leaped fervid into flame;
   Careless of queenhood, crowned and sanctified,
   Careless of honor and imperial fame,
   Broken beneath her sorrow and her shame
   That swept her spirit like a mighty wave,
   Straightway to her dead lover's side she came,
   That, love consummate lost, she yet might save
One moment of pure passion from the loveless grave.

At length the sad Queen sighed and raised her eyes,
   Heavy with grieving. The long night was past;
   The stars were pallid in the wan, white skies;
   A little wind stirred in the trees that cast
   Faint, trembling shadows on the flowers, massed
   In ghostly beauty, that beneath them lay;
   In the swift dawning seemed the heaven vast,
   Vacant and comfortless and cold and gray,
Stripped of the splendor of the night, unclothed with day

Weary she rose, and with the day her loss,
   Passion and pain and grief seemed ages old.
   Against the flushing dawn a chapel cross
   Flashed on a sudden into flaming gold;
   Slowly and heavily the great bell tolled;
   Faintly the singing of the nuns arose,
   Distant, ethereal and clear and cold,
   Fraught with the stillness of eternal snows,
With rest, long ease, content, comfort and sweet repose,

Bringing her heart a hope of refuge dim
    Beneath the shadow of a convent wall,
    With but the throb of some majestic hymn
    Or burst of organ melody to fall
    Across the silence. Tremulous and tall
    As a wind-shaken lily stood the Queen,
    Fronting the dawn, while solemnly o'er all
    The stir of morning rose the chant serene
Of those who came to bear him to his last demesne.

Yet as the black-robed nuns were drawing near,
    And the slow rhythm of their swelling song
    Rang out across the meadow, full and clear,
    Her old pride rose, imperiously strong
    From the vain sorrow of her vigil long.
    Love lay behind her, for the night was done
    That nor regret nor grieving could prolong,
    And a new strength and courage she had won
To meet the years of queenhood rising with the sun.

Swiftly and passionately at length she turned
    And with white fingers braided up her hair,
    Gathered the jewels that like embers burned
    And o'er her lover bending, tall and fair,
    Kissed him with lips that trembled with despair,
    With faith unspoken and with love untold.
    Then as the singing sounded on the stair
    And through the room the stately measure rolled,
The pale Queen rose and stood, imperially cold.

PART IV.
THE FOUR WINDS.
"Of the Four Seasons each has its own mood."
—Po Chu-i.

SUMMER.

Upon the tranquil bosom of the slumberous noon
   Lie the unmoving shadows of wide, spreading trees;
Luxuriant meadows, opulent with summer, swoon
Beneath the breathless spell of indolence and ease;
The hush of the full heat of noon is on the hill;
Blue dragon-flies hang shimmering above the stream;
The blossoms and the grasses droop; the birds are still;
Innumerable insects hum as in a dream;
In the faint, failing wind a leaf stirs languidly;
The notes of shrill cicadas into silence fall;
The purple clover bends beneath a clinging bee;
A butterfly dances on blazing wings; and over all
The smiting splendor of the noon sun flings a golden pall.

High in the heaven hangs a single cloud,
The glowing sunlight gathered to its breast.
There 'neath the spell of mighty magic bowed
The spirit fares on some transcendent quest
Through phantom shades to an untrodden town,
Where by strange headlands an old ocean sweeps,
And from huge heights dim, perilous paths lead down
To dire and unimaginable deeps.

Now is the time of earth's full flowering,
Summer's profusion, prodigally spent
In rich perfume and color, dowering
The teeming fields with languorous content.
Above their long leagues, warm and redolent,
Broods a sweet sense of being, scarce begun,
Of life eternal and omnipotent;
While through the leaves the wind's light ripples run,
And fruit in heavy clusters mellows in the sun.

AUTUMN.

Boisterous waves that laugh and leap
On the glistening rocks and the gleaming sand,
And swift blue shadows of clouds that sweep
Over the flaming autumnal land,
Set in a circle of flashing sea
Shaken with wild wind's ecstasy.

A glorious song the wind is singing,
Resounding music of sea and sky,
Of clamorous sea-gulls circling, swinging,
Of the hiss of waters washing high,
Of fugitive sails and the ocean flinging
A sun-lit splendor of flying foam
Where the crests of the surges curl and comb.

The clarion voice of the wind is calling
Over the heads of the listening hills
A burden of beauty beyond recalling,
Of hopes that fall as the leaves are falling,
Of sure foreknowledge of future ills.

The trumpet voice of the wind is thrilling
Through valleys vestured in golden grain,
Through orchards heavy with harvest, filling
The air with tumultuous summons, stilling
Futile regret and repining vain.

The passionate pulses of life are beating
Through meadows blazing with burnished gold
Faster and fiercer, and beauty, fleeting,
Brings deeper joy than it brought of old
When it rose at the summer's lightest greeting,
Ere its store was spent and its treasure told.

Yet as the music fails and falters,
And the wild wind dies with the dying sun,
And the fire sinks low on forsaken altars
Where life burned brightest, and one by one,

The leaves spin downward, there comes a grieving
For pure ambitions past achieving,
For visions vanished and deeds undone.

WINTER.

Harsh is the north wind's breath,
And harsh is death.
Huddled together in the searching air
The oaks stand gaunt and naked to the cold;
All things are bowed beneath a dark despair,
Are helpless, hopeless, tired and very old;
For the north wind's bitter breath
Is death.
The haggard trees are black against the west
Where a dull sunset smoulders sullenly,
While like a spent soul vainly seeking rest,
Foredoomed and fated to a fruitless quest,
Yet seeking endlessly
The wind goes by.
From bank to frozen bank
The long lake's face is blank;
And overhead
The sky is dead.

Now from the north comes the storm like a fierce wild thing
    that is lost,
Ruthlessly wrenching the boughs of the oaks in their agony
    tossed
Heavenward, writhing, imploring a respite, beseeching a rest
From the shuddering wildness of wind and the terror of tempest
    pressed
All but resistless against them. As bitter as death the blast
Mercilessly scourges the meadows, until like a dream that is
    passed,
The earth and the heavens have vanished, dead leaves in
    tumultuous flight,
And nothing remains but a wind that wails in a chaos of cold
    and night.

And now in utter silence, utter dark
The world lies stiffened, naked, stark;
No light, no sound beneath a barren sky,
Save for the black ice cracking suddenly.

All things shall come to this:
All wonder and all bliss,
All the swift passion of the hearts that beat
With sense of life unutterably sweet,
All song and laughter, all friendship and all love,
Delight in deed and dreaming, and above
The rest the rapture of creation,—all
Shall through the ages fail and fade and fall;
Until the earth, without one glowing spark
In all its livid leagues of frozen ground,
Shall whirl beneath the sky without a sound
Save for the black ice cracking in the dark.

SPRING.

Something is stirring within the earth;
Some spirit moves upon the air,
Prelude of melody and mirth,
Presage of spring's green, glorious birth
In the bosom of meadows brown and bare
And moist with the melting of snow.

The alders, crimson flushed, bend low
Beside the bank of the brimming stream,
Rippling its smooth and silent flow,
As roused from its long, dark, winter dream
With glint and glimmer and quiver and gleam
It hastens with swift and sweeping grace,
As though to a mystic meeting place.

The trees with pointed leaf buds swelling
Await in still expectancy
The wonder of the wind's foretelling,
The miracle of mirth to be.

For at the wind's light touch the world is rife
With swift, keen sense of newly wakened life,
Sweeter than full fruition of the spring.
And through the meadows like a flickering fire
Runs a fierce flaming of renewed desire
For the delight of beauty's blazoning,
For softening shadows and the brightening skies
Odor of earth and tender growing things,
The flash and flutter of the robins' wings;
The splendor of the spring that never dies.

The touch of the caressing wind that brings
A misty beauty to the budding spray
After the passage of a thousand springs
Shall give the glory that it gives to-day.

A time shall come when it shall not avail
To wake the world to burgeoning anew,
Yet shall the scent of blossoms never fail
Nor young leaves lose the freshness of their hue.

For when with us delight no longer dwells,
Then it shall pass to those great gulfs that lie
Beyond the stars that stand like sentinels
Around the little limits of our sky.

And other worlds shall rise beyond our ken
When we are given to darkness and to cold,
And there rejoicingly shall other men
Cherish the loves and dream the dreams of old.

After the dawning, they shall know the noon
And the sad splendor of the evening light,
And sink at last to silence like a tune
That throbbing dies to nothing in the night.

For countless stars beneath the great wind's breath
Shall leap to life and wax and wane and die;
Infinite life shall turn again to death,
And dark shall pass to dark eternally.

Yet though unnumbered suns, no longer glowing,
Silent beneath a silent heaven swing,
In the far depth of space the wind is blowing,
And on the verge of chaos it is spring.

PART V.
THE ALTAR CANDLE.
A Play in One Act.

DRAMATIS PERSONÆ:

LADY BEATRICE.
LORD GEOFFREY.
ANNE, the maid of Lady Beatrice.
A Jester.
A Nubian Mute.
Servants.

PLACE: A Baronial Castle.
TIME: Thirteenth Century.

ACT I.

Scene: A private apartment of Lady Beatrice. Back center, a prie-dieu of carved oak over which hangs a crucifix. Back left, a small door covered with a curtain. Back right, a larger door, the curtains of which are drawn, disclosing a passage. Right front, a door, beside which stands a table of black oak. On the table is a bronze gong. A large casement window (Left) which is open to the twilight. Before this a broad seat. Before the seat a footstool. On the walls, which are of stone, pieces of tapestry.

[*Before the curtain rises the Jester is heard off stage, singing.*]

"The moon I swear
Is not so fair
My lady love as you;"
So do men say
And vow that they
Will be forever true.

And for a while
The moon doth smile
And they are very true;
Yet love is blind
And soon they find
Another star will do.

[*The curtain rises, discovering Anne, and servants who are arranging the room, bringing candles, etc.*]

ANNE.

Make haste! make haste! Has not the merry spring
Set your old bones to dancing? What, so slow!
There's none of you in love, or else your feet
Would move in livelier measure.

[*Enter first servant with a dish of fruit.*]

First Servant.
      Here is fruit.

ANNE.

The table yonder.
  [*To second servant who is setting down a candle.*]
                Marry! Have you wits?
Set it not there.
  [*To third servant.*]
            Fetch you more candles.
  [*To second servant who is setting down the candle another place.*]
            So.
  [*She goes to the casement and blows a kiss to the moon*]
You are enough for lovers; we can kiss
Without a better light.

FOURTH SERVANT.

            Here is the wine,
A right good vintage. I could play the lord,
And do it well too, warmed with such a drink.

ANNE.

  [*Laughing and shutting the casement.*]
Peace! put it down.
  [*She crosses to the table and rearranges the fruit and wine; she takes an apple from the dish and holds it up as though to admire its bright color.*]
  [*Enter the Jester.*]
  [*He comes up stealthily behind Anne and kisses her. Dropping the apple she turns and administers a sounding box on the ear. The Jester retreats hastily pursued by Anne.*]
  [*Exit Jester.*]
  [*Anne stands vigorously rubbing off his kiss.*]
  [*A servant replaces the apple beside the dish.*]

[*Anne looks through the door (R) then she turns to the servants.*]

Enough, enough! 'Tis well;
The room will do now; get you gone.

[*Exeunt servants (Back).*]
[*Enter Geoffrey (R).*]

ANNE.

[*With deep curtsey.*]

My Lord.

[*While he advances, looking about the room, Anne draws the curtains at the back.*]

GEOFFREY.

I sought her Ladyship.

ANNE.

[*Coming forward.*]

None else, my Lord?

GEOFFREY.

Now, by my faith, I did not seek you, Anne!
Shall but a kiss or two bind me forever?

[*The Jester's face appears between the curtains.*]

ANNE.

I would not bind you, for I know you true;
Yet for a token that mayhap will keep
The memory of me bright within your heart,
When you are gone to-morrow to the wars,
I cut this lock off; guard it well, my Lord.

GEOFFREY.

[*Laughing.*]

Nay, keep your tresses, they become you better!

ANNE.
'Tis but a little token of the love,
The lasting love we feel.

GEOFFREY.
I feel it not.
What could have been between us but a love
Brief as the swallow's mating in the spring?

ANNE.
My Lord, you promised—

GEOFFREY.
What are promises
When spring is in the air? They are but part
Of the ephemeral love that gives them birth,
And die when love dies.

ANNE.
Are yours dead, my Lord?

GEOFFREY.
Dead.

ANNE.
[*Falling on her knees and grasping Geoffrey by the cloak*
Oh, my Lord! Then give them life again!
I am not what you think me, quickly won,
Yielding my heart to every passing smile.
My Lord! my Lord! My love is not for spring
But for eternity.

GEOFFREY.
[*Drawing away.*]
Be silent, girl.
Are you a child that reaches for the moon?

ANNE.
Geoffrey!
   [*The Jester's face disappears.*]

GEOFFREY.
[*Moving toward the door.*]
           Be but content to know the moon
Is far above your reach, and you may find
Some comfort in its beams.

ANNE.
Geoffrey!

GEOFFREY.
Farewell.

[*Exit Geoffrey (Back).*]
[*Anne remains on her knees weeping. She raises her head
   and listens; then she rises hastily and exit (Back).*]
[*Enter Beatrice (R).*]
[*She sees the curtain moving, and watches it for a
   moment; then she crosses to the casement and throws
   it open. The moonlight streams in.*]

BEATRICE.
The moon is on the meadows like a spell,
Deep as desire and magical as love.
   [*She gazes out for a moment, smiling. Then she strikes
      once on the gong and sinks back into the casement
      seat.*]
   [*Enter the Jester who approaches inquiringly. She motions
      him to the footstool.*]
   [*There is a short silence.*]

BEATRICE.
Sir Jester, have you ever been in love?

JESTER.
Pray you, my Lady, for my poor head's sake
Ask me some simple thing, as, "Are you well?"
Or "Have you dined?" or "Is your doublet warm?"
Some question that a downright "yes" or "no"
Will answer; but in love—truly love seems
As various as the many-colored bow
Hanging 'twixt sun and storm. For if by "love"
My Lady means delight in good hot soup,
Or fondness for a bed of clean dry straw,
Why then I am most thoroughly in love,
And may God keep me in that mind. Amen.
But if my Lady means a languishing
In some soft-cushioned moonlit casement seat,
With idly straying hands and dreaming eyes
Why then I know it not.

BEATRICE.
[*Laughing softly.*]
What think you of it?
Is it a thing that you would choose to have?

JESTER.
Indeed, 'tis pretty, and gives rise no doubt
To blushes, little catchings of the breath,
Sweet whispers, woeful sighs, and hands soft pressed,
And tuneful madrigals; yet this same love
So greatly undermines the appetite,
That I'll have none of it.

BEATRICE.
[*Dreamily.*]
Yet to the world
It gives a magic and a beauty greater
Than sun or moon or light of any star.

JESTER.
Truly there's magic in it.

BEATRICE.
                And content,
Comfort, and marvelously sweet repose,
Strong with the strength of faith. As when one moves
Through a thick forest, dark and overgrown,
And comes at length upon an open spot
Where the clear, smiting sunshine cleaves apart
The tangled trees, and makes a place of light
And warmth and freedom; so I found my love,
And in it found content.

                JESTER.
                Yes, for a time.
But love is always setting like the sun.
Men are forever false for all their vows,
And only God can know their constancy.—
Once, as the legend runs, there lived a maid
Fair as a summer day, fair even as you,
"The Lady of the Candles" she was called;
And in her heart love like rich music swelled
Harmoniously, and life was sweet; until
One whispered that her lover was untrue,
And told a tale of lust and treachery,
Troubling her utter purity of soul.
Yet in her meekness she but murmured, "God
Shall judge, not I"; and bade her lover come
And in the chapel by the altar steps,
Where the blessed candles burned beside the cross,
By ordeal prove his love. "Choose one," she said;
"God will direct your choice, and I shall know
Your faith or your inconstancy." He chose.
Then with soft laughter from her lightened heart
She said, "I never doubted you." And yet
Methinks the tale was not entirely false.

                BEATRICE.
You jest well, fool; and knowing naught of love,
Perchance there lies the measure of your folly;

For I have found a lover without flaw
To mar his honor.

JESTER.
Then your Ladyship
Has better eyes than I—or not so good.
I have seen sights, for none regarded me,
The fool; and truly it hath made me wonder
Who best becomes the motley; all the maids
So simple, trusting, and so lily pure;
And all the men, the perfect knights-at-arms,
Speckless and spotless—swift and passionate love—
Then a new face, a pair of redder lips—

> [*He breaks off with a shrug. Beatrice makes a gesture of disgust.*]

Nay, there is no one pure in all the court,
Saving my Lady Beatrice.

BEATRICE.

[*Softly.*] And my Geoffrey.

JESTER.

[*Tuning his guitar and not heeding Beatrice's remark.*]
For even Anne, my Lady's maid, hath proved
No wiser than the others, and hath found
That there's no trusting lovers' promises,
However great a lord the lover is;
For I had come to seek your Ladyship
To this same room, but a brief hour agone,
And found Anne pleading and his Lordship cold;
And when she fell before him, grasped his cloak,
And clung to him with desperate, clutching hands,
Hands he had fondled not so long ago,
He drew away impatiently, denied
His love for her and left her weeping there.
"Geoffrey!" she cried—

BEATRICE.

[*Starting up with a cry.*]
Geoffrey!

JESTER.

[*Laughing.*]
I marvel not
My Lady finds it scarce believable,
A likely story for a fool to tell.
Yet on mine honor as a fool, the girl
Spoke eloquently of passion and of vows,
Talked of remembrance and eternal love,
As though a lady; cut a lock of hair
For him to cherish as a thing of worth.
Yet was his Lordship merry; "Loose me, girl.
Put up your tresses, they become you better.
Are you a child that reaches for the moon?"

BEATRICE.

Sirrah, now by God's truth you smart for this!
Torture will teach you to control your tongue!

JESTER.

[*Falling on his knees.*]
Pardon, my Lady, pardon for God's sake!
What said I to offend your Ladyship?
'Twas but a fool's tongue, talking foolishly.

BEATRICE.

Here! Down upon your knees before the altar.
Take you the Book, and as you hope for Heaven
Swear you to speak the truth! What saw you here
Between my Lord and Anne?

JESTER.

Now as I hope
That Christ will pardon me my many sins,

I came by chance on Anne and my Lord Geoffrey.
Anne begged him to be true, fell at his feet
Better to plead her passion; he drew back
Before her groping fingers, and denied
His love for her; and then she cried his name;
He laughed and left her; as she cried again—

BEATRICE.

Enough. 'Tis well you tell your tale so pat,
Or else not all the oaths in earth or Heaven
Would have availed to save you! Get you gone.
 [*Exit Jester (R).*]
 [*Beatrice stands motionless for a moment, then in a passion of grief she throws herself on her knees befor
   the altar, and finally falls prostrate.*]
 [*Enter Anne (R).*]

ANNE.

My Lady!

BEATRICE.

Give me your arm.
 [*Supported by Anne she rises and sinks into a chair.*]
A little wine.

ANNE.

[*Pouring the wine.*]
What ails my Lady? Shall I fetch a leech?

BEATRICE.

Nay, nay, no leech; 'tis but a dream that's broken;
For some of us have dreams, dreams that we shape
Of heart's desire, and fashion tenderly
Of hope and high ambition and pure faith.
Yet dreams are full of sorrow, mark you that
And rest content with the dull, waking world.
 [*She rouses herself and looks attentively at Anne.*]

'Tis well for you that you fixed not your heart
Upon some shining mark you found too high
For your attainment, or flung down your love
At some man's feet for him to trample on,
Heeded his words or thought his promises
Would bind him longer than his fancy pleased;
So you are not heart-stricken, desolate
But—

    [*Anne, whose emotion has been increasing throughout Beatrice's speech, bursts into tears.*]

    Weeping Anne? Is no one without sorrow?
Tell me! Mayhap your grief may yet be cured.
What is it? A trinket lost? or a kiss stolen
In the passage by a bearded man-at-arms?

ANNE.

Nay, there's no man-at-arms nor page, my Lady!
No groom nor porter, no, nor veriest scullion,
That would so meanly serve me as—my Lord!
Oh! I have heard him eloquently talk
Of Launcelot and Tristram and the rest,
And say that all true knights should follow them
In "cleaving to one love"; and so he came
Full of sweet vows of everlasting love—
And I am fair enough for him to love—
How should I know they were as false as Hell?
His promises, his knightly promises!

BEATRICE.

[*Starting up.*]

Hark to me, Anne! I have been bitter wronged,
As you have, too, poor girl, by one I loved,
Honored and trusted beyond all the world.
I thought once that I was above all grief,
Chosen and set apart for happiness,
Yet God perceived my vanity, and God
Doth make us suffer dearly for our sin.—
Yet for the sin of others, that, methinks,

We need not suffer tamely nor endure;
And I will not endure it—yet my love
Cries like a wild thing that will not be still.
And I have none to counsel me, save God
Distant beyond my reach.—Yet I remember
Something the Jester told me of a trial,
Where God decreed forgiveness, mercy.—Anne!
Fetch me two candles from the chapel, two
That have been blessed, one white, the other red.

>   [*Exit Anne (B).*]
>   [*Beatrice strikes twice on the gong.*]
>   [*Enter a Nubian Mute (R).*]

>   BEATRICE.

Sirrah, have you a dagger? Can you strike
Swiftly and certainly?

>   [*The Nubian strides to the table, points to the apple beside the dish and drives his dagger through it with such force that the dagger stands quivering in the table. As Beatrice nods her approval he plucks it out.*]

                        Then look you there.
Behind that curtain lies a passageway
That leads directly to the castle gate;
Stand at the foot of the dark, winding steps,
And watch until I summon you again.
If in your vigil someone comes who bears
A candle, mark the color; if 'tis red,
Strike suddenly the bearer to the heart,
I care not whether it be man or maid,
Stranger or one you know; but if one comes
Who carries a white candle, let him pass
And touch him not. Take heed you do not fail.
If a red candle brings not certain death
To one who carries it, then you shall feel
The thumbscrew and the rack. Go; make no sound.

>   [*Exit Nubian (L).*]
>   [*Enter Anne with the candles (B).*]

BEATRICE.
Set them before the crucifix. Enough.
Tell my Lord Geoffrey I would see him here.
> [*Exit Anne (B).*]
> [*Beatrice stands for a moment looking at the candles; then she changes their position so that the red one is nearest the passage. She kneels and prays; she rises and seems on the point of changing them back again, when*]
> [*Enter Geoffrey (R).*]

You called me, Beatrice?

BEATRICE.

[*With dignity.*]
My Lord, I did.

GEOFFREY.
Pardon. Your Ladyship! I did not know
That you were "sir-ing" me.—What mood is this?
Truly methought you were not like the rest
Shifting and changing with each passing breath,
Now laughing, now in tears. Nay Beatrice,
Your heart has ever been a place of peace,
A refuge, a retreat, a sanctuary,
Where I might come to seek repose and strength,
Sure of a constant welcome.

BEATRICE.
Good my Lord,
A woman's heart has many hidden chambers;
It may be that my Lord has never been
Beyond the ante-room.

GEOFFREY.
Then I would go
Freely through every spacious gallery,
Learn the rich furnishings of every room,

The treasures of each alcove, and at length
By silken, hushed and winding passages
Come to the inmost shrine, your heart of hearts,
And in that place of worship kneel and pray.

BEATRICE.

Why then, my Lord, it would not be amiss
To take some heed to come with a pure heart.

GEOFFREY.

"Come with a pure heart!" 'Tis impossible;
I am no marble image of perfection.
Think you a man goes spotless through the world?
No, I come stained with dirt of marketplace,
Mire of the highway, blood of battlefield
Where I have bled for you, my Beatrice.

BEATRICE.

How may I then requite you for your wounds?

GEOFFREY.

You know full well, my Beatrice; give to me
No counsel of perfection, but your love;
That brings me absolution. Let your love
Wash me a perfect white, and keep me so.
I shall not falter, Beatrice, for a knight
Cleaves ever to one love—

> [*The Nubian in the passage accidentally drops the dagger; a ringing clash of steel is heard.*]
> [*Beatrice starts; her expression hardens.*]
> [*Geoffrey, who is on one knee before her, springs up and draws his sword.*]

GEOFFREY.
    What sound was that?

BEATRICE.
   [*Laughing nervously.*]
Some novice guardsman, careless of his pike,
Or courtier overcome with wassailing.

GEOFFREY.
   [*Listening for a moment longer, and then sheathing his sword.*]
I pray you, Beatrice, let your perfect love
Give me an arm like Arthur, and a sword
As mighty as the great Excalibur;
For with your favor on mine helm I'd ride
Resistless to the Holy Sepulchre,
Though every Turk and every fiend of Hell
Should cross my path to stay me!

BEATRICE.
                    Good my Lord,
Press me no more. Truly I cannot say
Whether I love you; God will show right soon.
A woman's heart may not be lightly won
   [*Aside.*]
Or being won may not be lightly lost.

GEOFFREY.
   [*Half angrily.*]
I crave your pardon that I dared to think
That you might love. Have you no more to say
Before I bid your Ladyship farewell?

BEATRICE.
This. That to-morrow if you *should* go forth
To fight the Infidel—and safe return,
You find a warmer welcome. Rest content
My Lord with that.

GEOFFREY.
[*Bowing and turning to leave.*]
>You shall command in all.

BEATRICE.
[*Stopping him with a gesture.*]
Go not that way, my Lord, but privately
By mine own passage to the castle yard.
But it is dark and fearful! Take you then
One of those candles on the altar there.
Take it not carelessly, for it is blessed,
And haply may be fraught with deeper meaning
Than the mere lighting of a passageway.
Truly it might portend your life or death.

GEOFFREY.
[*Amused.*]
Why since a candle is so great a thing
I'll make my choice with due solemnity.
White! for your soul as pure as yonder moon
That makes all glorious the summer night;
Red! for the blood that pulses in your cheeks
And tells of a true heart; white for your hands
Fashioned for naught but tender cherishing,
Red for the warmth of your unswerving love.
Why then I'll take—

BEATRICE.
[*Greatly agitated.*]
>Geoffrey! My Lord!
[*Her glance falls on the fruit on the table.*]
>Some fruit?
To-morrow you will have no dainty fare.
[*In her excitement she offers him a half of the apple cl by the dagger.*]

GEOFFREY.
Grammercy, Beatrice; but I have supped.
[*He turns to the altar.*]

BEATRICE.
[*Almost hysterical.*]
Stay but a moment! See, the goblet! Come,
Pledge me your love in a deep draught of wine!
[*She fills the goblet with shaking hands.*]

GEOFFREY.
[*Holding it high.*]
I pledge thee mine unwavering constancy!
Thou art my morning and my evening star,
My lasting love and my most sure salvation!
[*He drinks; then he approaches the altar.*]
And so I take this one, red, passion red!
[*Beatrice, suppressing a scream, stands motionless. Geoffrey bows, kisses her hand and turns to leave, bearing the red candle; as he reaches the door she calls him.*]

BEATRICE.
Geoffrey!
[*Geoffrey puts down the candle, runs to her and embraces her passionately. For a time they stand silent in the shaft of moonlight.*]

GEOFFREY.
How sweet these lips are, Beatrice!
I have no words to tell my love, nor could
The eloquence of angels give the sum.

BEATRICE.
Silence is better, and a resting here.

GEOFFREY.

I sought you, Beatrice, as the knights of old
Sought for the Grail, that perfect, holy thing
Worth a long life of peril and of pain,
That yet to those who found it could not give
Such healing or such happiness as these.

[*Kissing her.*]

BEATRICE.

How empty seems the past now, and how strange!
How did I spend my days before I found
This love, the whole of life?

GEOFFREY.
                      Your hands, beloved,
Bestow a blessing of far greater worth
Than holiest benediction of the saints,
Nor from the gates of Paradise itself,
Opening to choiring of the cherubim,
Shines such a splendor as from these dear eyes;
Nor in the realm behind those glorious gates
Is comfort or delight as deep as this.

BEATRICE.

Deeper than Heaven. Have you loved me long?
For truly, I have loved since time began.

GEOFFREY.

Since I first saw you in the garden there,
Crocus and daffodil about your feet,
Above you apple-blossoms and young leaves
Making soft shadows on your hair, and you
Fairer than all the spring.

BEATRICE.
              As a flower lies
Through the long winter in the dark and cold

My heart lay stifled, until like the spring
You came and kindled it to life and love.

Geoffrey.

If I have come, I shall not pass like spring;
Nor will our passion live a summer's length
And die with dying foliage in the fall;
No, t'will outlive all seasons and all time,
As everlasting as the holy cross,
As steadfast as a candle ever burning
Before the image of a saint.

Beatrice.

[*Starting from him.*]
      The candle!

[*She turns and gazes at the red candle on the table, as the memory of her grief and shame comes back to her. Then she turns to Geoffrey, takes a ring from her finger and gives it to him.*]

We part now for a little; take this ring
Cherish and guard it like my love forever.

[*She takes the red candle and walks to the door of the passageway; then she turns.*]

And if perchance in some far future time
You think but for a moment of this hour,
Remember me as one who gave her heart
Completely to a perfect love and faith.

[*Exit Beatrice.*]
[*Geoffrey stands looking at the ring. A terrible sound, half shriek, half groan, is heard in the passage. Geoffrey draws his sword, rushes to the door and pulls apart the curtain; he stands for an instant as though paralyzed. Anne appears in the door (B) and the Jester (R). Then Geoffrey disappears down the passage*]

Curtain.

PRINTED IN THE UNITED STATES OF AMERICA

CPSIA information can be obtained
at www.ICGtesting.com
Printed in the USA
LVHW081025051120
670821LV00011B/251